# CAN THE BIBLE MEAN WHATEVER WE WANT IT TO MEAN?

Canon Anthony C. Thiselton

Research Professor of Christian Theology

Emeritus Professor of Christian Theology,
University of Nottingham
Canon Theologian of Leicester Cathedral and of
Southwell Minster

An Inaugural Lecture
Delivered at University College Chester
on 29 October 2004

Chester Academic Press

First published 2005
by Chester Academic Press
Learning Resources
University College Chester
Parkgate Road
Chester CH1 4BJ

Printed and bound in the UK by the
Learning Resources Print Unit,
University College Chester
Cover designed by the
Learning Resources Graphics Team
University College Chester

©Anthony C. Thiselton, 2005

All Rights Reserved
No part of this publication may be reproduced, stored in a retrieval system or transmitted in any form or by any means without the prior permission of the copyright owner, other than as permitted by current UK legislation or under the terms of a recognised copyright licensing scheme

A catalogue record for this publication is available from the British Library

# CAN THE BIBLE MEAN WHATEVER WE WANT IT TO MEAN?

**Introduction**

Like Julius Caesar's Gaul, and like many Sunday sermons, this lecture is divided into three parts. Part One concerns a shift in debates about the Bible some forty or fifty years ago from more traditional questions to keen controversies about interpretation. In this first part, I also introduce the nature and scope of what is technically hermeneutics as an essential resource for addressing our question.

In Part Two, we discuss some criteria for textual meanings, with six illustrative examples or case studies. Here I shall focus on more traditional resources that emerge within the framework of modernity, although I shall also consider the increasing impact of literary theory.

Part Three addresses the impact of postmodern perspectives. These affect biblical interpretation and Christian theology profoundly, for good or ill. The value of postmodern approaches remains keenly, often passionately, controversial in most university schools or departments.

I hope that such an approach will not disappoint expectations, which inaugural lectures may sometimes frustrate. I recall dutifully attending one in the Medical Faculty in Nottingham University. It was advertised as being on the subject of losing weight in the light of research on human metabolism. I had hoped for some esoteric tips on how to lose weight painlessly. However,

Can the Bible Mean Whatever We Want It to Mean?

the speaker spent the entire hour and a half on how to help the undernourished to gain weight.

## I. The Shift of Focus in the Debate about the Bible to Issues of Meaning and Interpretation, and the Nature and Scope of Hermeneutics as a Resource for Our Question

Up until the 1950s and 1960s, debates about the authority and use of the Bible often turned on a simplistic opposition between three supposedly competing sources of authority: the Bible, the Church and human reason.

However, many factors exposed the difficulty of viewing these as competing, rather than complementary, sources of authority. Richard Hooker, often regarded as a classic representative of Anglican theology, insisted that scripture, the tradition of the Church and reason function *together* as norms for doctrine and life, although within this plurality scripture holds primacy.

Many whom we might associate with a high doctrine of the Bible also draw on traditions of the Church and use rational argumentation for interpreting the Bible. Luther and Calvin do draw upon the traditions of the earlier Church Fathers, and both employ rational argument to defend their beliefs. This is likewise true of the apostle Paul. As Wolfhart Pannenberg observed, Paul could have spared himself considerable trouble if he had thought it enough simply to quote the Old Testament or to appeal to the Holy Spirit, but he took time to hammer out careful rational arguments (1971, pp. 34-35; cf. pp. 28-64).

Even those biblical scholars who attack biblical fundamentalism recognize, to cite James Barr, that to attend to scripture as an authoritative source of

## Can the Bible Mean Whatever We Want It to Mean?

doctrine and ethics is "analytical" or "internal" (to use Barr's words) to what it is to be a Christian (1980, p. 52). C. H. Dodd contrasts the *corporate and community witness* of the biblical writings with a narrower *individualism*. He writes: "We may well turn away from the narrow scene of individual experience of the moment, to the spacious prospect we command in the Bible. Here we meet with those whom we must acknowledge as experts in life .... Here also we trace the long history of a community which through good fortune and ill tested their belief in God .... This has delivered us from the tyranny of private impressions ..." (1928, pp. 298-9).

Finally, from a different direction, exponents of philosophical hermeneutics provide significant reappraisals of the relation between reason and tradition or authority. Hans-Georg Gadamer declares in his magisterial *Truth and Method*: "Authority ... rests on acknowledgement, and hence on an act of reason itself, which, aware of its own limitations, trusts to the better insight of others" (1989, p. 279).

Yet these more constructive statements do not clear away all difficulties. For it has not achieved very much if we accord to the Bible a unique authority as long as (to overstate the problem) we can find no two people who can agree about what biblical texts actually mean or how they are to be applied.

It is no accident that this change of focus to questions about interpretation coincided with a shift in biblical studies from the so-called biblical theology school, with its emphasis upon the unity of the Bible, to redaction criticism, which stressed its pluriformity. Can the Bible speak at all with a single, clear, coherent, voice? A number of writers offer a negative answer. One of the most

## Can the Bible Mean Whatever We Want It to Mean?

strident voices is that of Heikki Räisänen, who insists that the Bible cannot serve as a foundation for Christian theology, since it speaks with conflicting and contradictory voices and theologies (2001, pp. 227-249).

Conflicts of interpretations that carry social and political implications are the most notorious. Many stem from the nineteenth century. In 1864, Bishop J. H. Hopkins of Vermont asserted: "The Bible's defence of slavery is very plain .... Who are we that in our modern wisdom presume to set aside the Word of God" (p. 16). Needless to say, abolitionists held contrary interpretations of biblical passages.

A second controversial area is that of war. George W. Knight insists that: "The God and Father of Abraham, Isaac, Jacob ... and Jesus Christ instructed his people of old to wage war ... and to slay the enemy .... This makes it impossible to maintain that God prohibits the Christian from engaging in war" (1975, p. 4). The Brazilian liberation theologian Rubem Alves appeals to biblical precedents for action "subversive of the stability created by violence" on the part of a state (1969, p. 125). Exponents of Black hermeneutics have cited the Afrikaner draft constitution of 1942 that saw the conquest and acquisition of South African land by the African White Voortrekkers as a national calling "in obedience to God and his holy Word". Takatso Mofokeng coined the aphorism: "When the White man came to our country he had the Bible, and we had the land .... After prayer, the White man had the land, and we had the Bible" (1988, p. 34).

Examples and case studies are important but, before I cite more and the reasons behind them, it is time to comment briefly on the nature and scope of the discipline of hermeneutics as the area of resource for the present subject. The discipline emerged in the ancient world, but became a modern critical academic discipline only from the time of Schleiermacher. His writings on hermeneutics span 1805 – 1829[1]. In the late twentieth century, with the magisterial contributions of Hans-Georg Gadamer (1989), Emilio Betti (1967, 1972) and Paul Ricoeur (1970, 1992), hermeneutics has become an ever more complex, sophisticated and demanding multi-disciplinary area.

The prehistory of questions about interpretation began with Stoic debates about interpretations of Homer, with Rabbi Hillel's so-called seven rules of interpretation and with Philo, Irenaeus and Origen. Hermeneutics, however, denotes also critical reflection on processes of interpretation. In the second century, Irenaeus attacked gnostic writers for assimilating the language of the Bible to validate their beliefs, but only by taking biblical words or phrases out of their proper context and changing their meanings. It is as if they find a picture constructed from precious jewels: they wrench these jewels from their proper place, "take it … to pieces … re-arrange the gems, and so fit them together as to make them into the form of [a different picture]" (*Against Heresies,* book 1, trans. 1885). Irenaeus was ahead of his times. He anticipates the later Wittgenstein in distinguishing between language as such and specific *uses* of language.

Hermeneutics changed dramatically with Schleiermacher. The subject no longer remains merely an extension of philology, lexicography, grammar, biblical studies and theology. It now concerns the very nature of

---

[1] See Schleiermacher (1977).

human understanding and "the art of thinking". Schleiermacher insists that it becomes *philosophical*. It further involves the *social* dimension of interpersonal *communicative action.* Thereby, it transcends a merely "scientific" knowledge of texts and language. Person-to-person understanding entails what Schleiermacher calls a "divinatory" dimension.

In view of the constraints of time, I will summarise in the briefest possible outline five dimensions of modern critical multidisciplinary hermeneutics that, coincidentally, five of my publications illustrate.

(1) Hermeneutical enquiry explores the historical settings of biblical books, their genre, their purpose, theology and relation to today's world. I address these goals in my commentary on the Greek text of 1 Corinthians (2000). Research into the Roman background of Corinth, together with its archaeology and culture, sheds a flood of light on the meaning of numerous passages within this epistle. I shall shortly consider 6: 1-8 as offering an example of this. For readers of the epistle today, does the meaning of this chapter really turn on whether it is right to go to law?

(2) My volume *The Two Horizons* (1980) asks how the horizons that readers today bring with them to the text may actively *engage with* the horizons of the ancient biblical text. I argue that respect for the historical and theological distance and difference of the text prevents a premature assimilation of the two horizons. Apostles and first-century Christians, let alone the Old Testament patriarchs or prophets, are not simply replicas of a parish vicar or churchwarden. Yet the impossibility of assimilation should not suggest the impossibility of active engagement.

Can the Bible Mean Whatever We Want It to Mean?

An example may clarify the point. In my first chapter, I point out that the Parable of the Pharisee and the Tax Collector in Luke 18: 9-14 will be likely to remain bland and lack genuine engagement if we fail to recognise how 2000 years of Church and cultural tradition has made our perception of Pharisees entirely different from that of the original audience. The parable makes little impact today if we interpret its meaning as a predictable moral tale in which those whose religion is supposedly merely formal or even at times hypocritical are perceived as less likely to receive God's mercy than an outsider who truly repents. In fact, Jesus enticed his hearers into a narrative world in which a devout, committed person of faith boldly offers thanks for the opportunities he has to study and to practice God's law, while someone who manipulated the tax system for personal gain creeps guiltily into the back of the church. To their consternation, the audience hears the shocking verdict that God's declaration of mercy falls not upon the devout Pharisee, but upon the grasping Collector of Taxes. The hermeneutical dynamic of the story is primarily that of a narrative world into which an audience is enticed initially by the safe and familiar, only to find that the sovereign grace of God unexpectedly turns all their assumptions upside down. It is a parable of reversal.

(3) The subtitle of my book *New Horizons in Hermeneutics* (1992) identifies the third theme: *The Theory and Practice of Transforming Biblical Reading.* Anxieties about pluralities of meaning become exaggerated if we regard the Bible primarily and exclusively as a textbook of information, on the analogy of an engineering handbook, rather than a source of transformation. In the opening chapter of this volume, I argue that the Bible is no less

## Can the Bible Mean Whatever We Want It to Mean?

transformative than a substantial bequest from a will or the receipt of a love-letter. These are speech-acts.

But transformed into what? In ultimate terms, the Bible may transform readers into the image of Christ. But in the shorter term, it may transform the downcast to lift them up or the self-sufficient into recognition of their need. This might be construed by the unimaginative as an example of conflicting meanings, as if to direct one person to turn left and another to turn right constituted contradictory directions for travel, when each began from a different place.

(4) In *The Promise of Hermeneutics* (Lundin, Walhout, & Thiselton, 1999), I have drawn upon speech-act theory in linguistics as well as literary theory to illuminate narrative. One section explicitly addresses *polyphonic voices* and has immediate bearing on our subject. In literary theory, Mikhail Bakhtin has shown that Fyodor Dostoevsky more than once used the device of polyphonic voices in his novels (1973). In *The Brothers Karamazov* (1879-1880/1976, especially pp. 216-242), the "voice" of the author is not simply to be identified with the brother Ivan's voice of protest (as Camus believed) nor with the devout voice of the brother Alyosha (as Berdyaev implies). It is precisely the interplay and dialectic between several distinct voices that conveys the burden of the novel as a polyphonic harmony, unresolved into a mere single note.

A response to the problem of evil can never be packaged into a single voice. Hence, the Book of Job does not function to provide a single, univocal, pre-packaged "answer", but invites readers to share in the *dialectical wrestling* that occurs between the voices of Job, of one or more of the friends, of the editorial narrative, and, yes, even of God. Revelation entails the dialectic of the *whole*.

Can the Bible Mean Whatever We Want It to Mean?

Räisänen (2001, pp. 227-249) misses the point that Christian theology emerges painfully out of such dialectical wrestling, struggle and labour.

(5) Finally, since the end of the 1960s, hermeneutics has faced the challenges of postmodernity and has sought to learn from this encounter. I entered this debate initially in 1995 in *Interpreting God and the Postmodern Self,* subtitled *On Meaning, Manipulation and Promise.* Here I address *manipulative* interpretation of the Bible and the anti-theistic challenges of Friedrich Nietzsche and others on the use of reading strategies of disguise to promote power and self-affirmation under the guise of claiming to convey truth. Nietzsche comments: "The salvation of the soul – in plain language, the world revolves around me!" (1895/1990, aphorism 43). In more radical versions of postmodern hermeneutics, texts do little more than mirror the community of interpreters, now imprisoned within their own prior horizons. Interpretation becomes self-affirmation. Yet for Martin Luther, scripture as the Word of God reveals its cutting edge most sharply when it confronts us "as our adversary" (Latin, *adversarius noster*).

Gadamer (1989), Ricoeur (1970, 1992) and Betti (1967, 1972), the three greatest hermeneutical theorists of the late twentieth century, would agree with many postmodernists that hermeneutics has as its goal not the *"mastery"* of texts by imposing upon them some prior conceptual grid constructed by the reader, but a patient process of listening that seeks to hear the text or the Other speak on its own terms and in its own right. Gadamer speaks of hermeneutics as a discipline of the ear rather than the mouth. Betti believes that hermeneutics should be an obligatory subject in every university, because it nurtures tolerance, patience and openness to the Other to address us *as* the Other (1967, p. 21; 1972, p. 7). It differs from the methods of science and technology, the methods of mastery, which are appropriate enough for *knowing objects,* but inappropriate, blind, and self-willed for understanding texts and persons. *Patient listening* is the way of hermeneutics.

## 2. Resources for Assessing Biblical Meanings Within the Framework of Modernity: With Six Illustrative Examples

I shall explore six case studies, with comments on how each relates respectively to different resources of hermeneutics. The first is a relatively trivial example, but the absence of any vested interest facilitates openness to assess the issues. Further, this example reveals the ambiguous logical currency of the word "can" in the question: "Can the Bible mean whatever we want it to mean?"

(1) In Gen. 31: 49 (NRSV), Laban exclaims: "The Lord watch between you and me, when we are absent one from the other". Numerous devout Christians have used this text as a fond commitment of a loved one or a dear friend to God as they part for a period of time. It is used as a kind of blessing and commitment each of the other to God's protection.

Is this what the verse means? One writer call this "an unmeant" meaning. The Hebrew verse for *to watch* used here, צפה (*tsaphah*) *can* bear this meaning, but more often denotes *watching out*, typically for an enemy. The context from Genesis 29 onwards, however, portrays Jacob and Laban playing one dastardly trick after another against

## Can the Bible Mean Whatever We Want It to Mean?

each other, each worse than the one before. These range from cheating the other out of flocks of sheep to ensuring that the other is lumbered with the wrong wife. I can never forget reading the vivid Hebrew of Gen. 29: 25 as a text for my first degree. Jacob had married, he thought, his beloved Rachel, presumably heavily veiled, and took her to bed. The Hebrew reads, בבקר הנה־הוא לאה (*bhabhoker hinneh-hu Leah*): "And in the morning: behold! [or choose your expletive] - Leah!" So would Laban say to Jacob: "I do hope the Lord will lovingly take care of you while we are parted?" Laban means: "May the Lord glue his eyes on you and avenge me if you try another trick!"

So *can* this text mean what a pietist reading suggests? It *can*, if this is how a community of pietists uses it. But is this a *textual* meaning when everything in the context excludes such a meaning on the part of the text, the narrator, and the speaker?

A huge controversy arises here between advocates of traditional historical-grammatical and contextual exegesis and those who approach the Bible purely in literary terms or as postmodern interpreters. Until recently, most biblical scholars took the former for granted. But over the last twenty years, a growing number want to give greater emphasis to the role of the reader. This coheres with reader-response theory, autobiographical criticism and most versions of postmodernism. Sometimes, an additional political agenda motivates this shift. Authors are viewed as an elite who shape what readers think. But if *all* readers are, in effect, co-authors, only a single egalitarian reading community exists. Some, further, deconstruct a biblical or literary canon as elitist and anti-democratic. At all events, readers determine the meaning.

Can the Bible Mean Whatever We Want It to Mean?

In reply, I believe that *genre* is a key critical factor. Reader-response theorists have a point when we are considering what Lotman (1977) and Umberto Eco (1979, pp. 4-33; 1984, pp. 68-86) call "open" texts. These are often, but not always, parables, poetry, hymnic texts or psalms, and sometimes parts of the wisdom literature. Lotman and Eco call them "productive" texts, because they may serve to tease, seduce, and provoke the reader into active thought. But many texts in the Bible are *not* poetic, symbolic, parabolic or hymnic. They are *prophetic, apostolic, didactic, creedal, or historic reports*, and these are *transmissive, communicative,* texts. When Paul writes: "I received from the Lord what I also handed on to you as of first importance, that Christ died for our sins according to the scriptures, that he was buried, and that he was raised ... " (1 Cor. 15: 3[2]), this is part of a *communicative, transmissive*, linguistic act. As in most didactic communication, the utterance is operative when the "receiver" grasps what the "sender" sends through the media of source, code, contact, message and receiver. It entails what John Searle (1983, pp. 19-20, pp. 144-159) and Jonathan Culler (1975, p. 137, p. 247; 1981, p. ix, p. 5, p. 55, p. 95) call reader-competency.

(2) In 1 Cor. 6: 1-8, Paul declares: "If one of you has a dispute with another, how dare he go to law before a pagan court "(v. 1). "Must Christian go to law with Christian? ... You suffer defeat by going to law" (vv. 6-7[3]). A widespread assumption is that these verses condemn going to law. But is this the point at issue for twenty-first

---

[2] The author's translation; see Thiselton (2000).

[3] Ibid.

## Can the Bible Mean Whatever We Want It to Mean?

century readers? Historical and archaeological research demonstrate beyond doubt that, although it was a Greek city in the geographical sense, the constitution, politics, law, and government of Corinth were modelled on Rome, not Greece, in Paul's day. Julius Caesar refounded it as a Roman *colonia* in 44 BC. From the time of Paul to that of Hadrian, virtually all inscriptions are in Latin, not Greek. This bears on our passage, for while Roman *criminal* law was relatively impartial, *civil* lawsuits operated differently. It was expected that both parties to a dispute would offer incentives to the judge (and when applicable the jury) to grant a favourable verdict. This might be an unashamed financial bribe, or the benefit of business contacts, invitations to prestigious social events, gifts of property or slaves, or whatever.

In such a situation, only rich and influential Christians would consider it worth taking a fellow Christian to the civil courts. Paul attacks not a responsible use of law; he himself appeals to Roman law. He attacks the underhand *manipulation* of a fellow Christian through superior wealth, power, social influence or business networks. This amounts to using indirect force to gain what is coveted. Prohibition of resort to law as such is not what these verses *mean*. They can mean whatever we want them to mean only if we fly in the face of reason and responsibility, and reject all contextual constraints.

(3) Another example comes from 1 Cor. 7: 1. Many misunderstood this verse until the Revised English Bible and New Revised Standard Version, both of 1989, placed part of it in quotation marks: "It is a good thing for a man not to have intercourse with a woman". For centuries, in the absence of quotation marks, this view was imposed upon Paul. There is no clear way of signalling quotation

## Can the Bible Mean Whatever We Want It to Mean?

marks in the Uncial MSS of Hellenistic Greek, but once we insert quotation marks the argument of 7: 1-7 runs smoothly and coherently. Meanwhile, the Authorised Version of 1611, the Revised Version of 1881, the Revised Standard Version of 1946, the New English Bible of 1961, and even the New International Version of 1979 translate the Greek without inverted commas.

There are a number of clear examples of quotations in 1 Corinthians. The most widely recognised is 6: 12: "All things are lawful", or (REB) "I am free to do anything". This served as a Corinthian buzz-phrase that Paul takes up, but immediately qualifies: "But not everything does good". Others come in 6: 13; 8: 1; 8: 4; 10: 23; and probably elsewhere. Can mere punctuation marks change an established meaning? These proposals have been fully tested by historical, linguistic, and syntactical or grammatical research. These verses cannot mean simply what we want them to mean, unless we renounce attention to context and reason.

All the same, are these the most serious causes of disagreements about meanings? Our next two examples illustrate the claim of Robert Morgan (1988) that the most serious conflicts of interpretation arise not so much from differences of exegesis, but from differences of *method*. Morgan argues that the impact of literary theory has transposed the debate into a new key.

One positive outcome has been a new evaluation of what were traditionally regarded as clumsy constructions of "doublets", namely dual narratives of events drawn from two different sources, as if by scissors-and-paste editors. As *historical* reports they sometimes seem to stand in irreconcilable tension with each other.

Can the Bible Mean Whatever We Want It to Mean?

(4) In *The Art of Biblical Narrative* (1981), Robert Alter compares the two accounts of the call of David to kingship as literary texts. In 1 Sam. 15-16, God charges Samuel to find David and to anoint him as King in Saul's place. 1 Sam. 16: 13 concludes with David's anointing in his home. Chapters 17-31, however, recount a series of twists and turns as David arrives at Saul's court, fights Goliath and feuds with Saul. Many assume that an editor has clumsily sown together two sources. By contrast, Alter reminds us that, in literary theory, the deployment of more than one "point of view" is a standard tool for narrative composition. Two such accounts need not be contradictory. One recounts the call of David from *the point of view* of divine call and providence; the other traces the steady implementation of the call "from the point of view of the everyday hurly-burly of human life". The narrator uses stereoscopic lenses.

(5) A part-parallel example from the New Testament concerns the vexed question of comparing sequences and chronologies in the first three Gospels. Complex theories have emerged to account for certain differences. However, in literary theory Seymour Chatman (1978) and Gerard Genette (1980) have produced important work on narrative time. Flashbacks, flash-forwards and other restructuring of narrative time are necessary devices for narrative. You could not *tell* an Agatha Christie or P. D. James detective story if the story *began* with a fully transparent account of the crime. What would be left of the story to tell? The dramatic sequence must begin *after* the crime, if necessary using flashbacks.

Many believe that Mark uses three different tempos of narrative time in his Gospel. From Chapter 1 to 8: 26, the tempo is very rapid. The Greek often uses *euthus* as a rapid

## Can the Bible Mean Whatever We Want It to Mean?

connective between episodes, denoting "immediately" or "the very next thing that happened". Jesus rushes on to his destiny. In 8: 27-38, Peter confesses his Messiahship at Caesarea Philippi, and from here to the Passion narrative the tempo slows to a moderate pace. Finally, in the last section, Mark narrates the Passion events in slow motion. This, he says, is what everything led up to; this is what it was all for.

Once we conceive of the differences between clock time and narrative time, some of the older theories about clumsy discrepancies may become obsolete. This is no special pleading. The sociology of time sheds light on much in human life: on patterns of employment, social relations and economics. Our recent Church of England Doctrine Commission Report, *Being Human* (2003), traces the theological significance of some of these factors, and I explore narrative time in *The Promise of Hermeneutics* (Lundin, Walhout, & Thiselton, 1999), as well as more briefly in *New Horizons* (1992).

On the basis of reader-response theory, however, literary theory may seem to suggest that the Bible *can* sometimes mean whatever we want it to mean. Moreover, biblical texts often project "narrative worlds" into which they invite or seduce readers, but only to tease the reader into active thought, and often to reverse initial understanding into a subsequent one. Does this not entail a certain fluidity and openness of meaning and understanding?

(6) In the Parable of the Labourers in the Vineyard in Matt. 20: 1-16, we witness the good fortune of those who receive a full day's wage for working only one hour in the cool of the evening. We wonder how much *more* those who have laboured for twelve hours and borne the heat

## Can the Bible Mean Whatever We Want It to Mean?

and burden of the day will receive! With them, we wait with baited breath. Then, with them, we are disgusted and appalled when they receive the same. It is not fair! Yes, says Jesus, divine grace does cause offence. It eclipses justice; but if we reflect on what makes us angry, this is not that the hardworking receive less than they deserve, but that God shows extra generosity to the undeserving. The hermeneutical function is not that of an intellectual treatise on grace. It draws the hearer into a narrative world that makes us feel the shock of grace in our very bones.

When he says: "He who has ears to hear, let him hear" (Mark 4: 9 [RSV]), Jesus means neither "make whatever you like of this" nor "the meaning is fully determinate; it is cut and dried". He invites a responsible judgement from hearers that may involve a series of revisions of understanding. Hermeneutical understanding, in contrast merely to semantic meaning, frequently entails long processes of listening, patience and even openness to transformation. Some of our initial ways of understanding the question: "Can the Bible mean whatever we want it to mean?" may appear naive in the light of such a complex and sometimes meandering process.

Often, we can provide a clear and decisive answer to the question: "What does the text *not* mean?" Responsible historical, contextual, and grammatical exegesis frequently excludes certain meanings. Nevertheless, in positive terms the problem is more complex. Paul Ricoeur brilliantly sums up the dual task of hermeneutics when he observes: "Hermeneutics seems to me to be animated by this double motivation: *willingness to suspect, willingness to listen*; vow of rigor, vow of obedience" (1970, p. 27). Hermeneutical suspicion is necessary to prevent our reading texts merely in ways that serve self-interest. This sets up idols, idolatrous constructs of our own making. A hermeneutic of retrieval permits us to listen to what speaks from beyond our world of interests. This may involve what Ricoeur calls listening to symbols that point beyond themselves to a transcendent reality. They point to "the Other".

## 3. Doing Away With Idols: Hermeneutics Within the Framework of Postmodernity

I have already observed that Friedrich Nietzsche, the precursor of postmodernity before its time, insisted that religious people, especially their leaders, purport to find truth in the Bible, but in practice use manipulation and disguise to affirm the self and to gain power over others. "The salvation of the soul" - in plain language: "The world revolves around me"; "The one who repents" - in plain language: "The one who submits to the priest" (1895/1990, aphorism 43).

In a number of more recent research articles, to be published in 2005 in a volume of collected works, I have argued that the European postmodernism of Nietzsche, Foucault, Derrida and others can assist us in detecting inauthentic manipulative interpretations designed to promote self-interest. On the other hand, the neo-pragmatic postmodernity of such American thinkers as Richard Rorty (1998) and Stanley Fish (1989, pp. 1-33), against all their claims to offer a "radical" hermeneutics, have the effect, in my judgment, of undermining the very purpose of hermeneutics. If the only viable criterion of meaning is that which coheres with what their reading community regards as conducive to "progress", all interpretation becomes corporate self-affirmation.

Can the Bible Mean Whatever We Want It to Mean?

I confess that I find it extremely difficult to sum up in this last ten or fifteen minutes what I should like to say about the relation between postmodernity and biblical interpretation. This has been the subject of many lectures and many pages of writing. Presumably we need to begin with some rough and ready account of what we mean by postmodernity. David Lyon (1994, pp. 6-7) and Graham Ward (2001, p. xiv) try to distinguish between *postmodernity* and *postmodernism*. Lyon sees *postmodernism* primarily as a philosophical and intellectual movement that rejects the rationalism of the secular Enlightenment and the privileging of scientific method, let alone a scientific world-view, as the universal model of knowledge or understanding. This carries with it a suspicion of all systems and universals. By contrast, he sees *postmodernity* as a social phenomenon, socially constructed. It projects a virtual-reality world, not built by the solid world of engineering, building-science, or geography, but projected by the "soft" reality of information technology, consumer profiles, mass advertising and the media, and the purchasing power of particular socio-economic groups.

In practice, however, many writers use these two terms interchangeably. The most widely used definition of postmodernity is that of Jean-François Lyotard, namely an attitude of "incredulity towards metanarratives". A metanarrative, or "grand narrative", is a universalising narrative or story that seeks to subsume other stories and claims to truth or value within its own framework. The grand narratives of high modernity are typically those of Darwinianism, Freudianism and Marxism. These seek to impose explanatory or validating criteria upon the world as a whole. This introduces the first of several themes in

## Can the Bible Mean Whatever We Want It to Mean?

postmodernism selected here since they relate closely to hermeneutics.

(1) This approach remains intensely suspicious of any attempt to interpret the Bible as offering definitive meanings that provide an account of all reality and universal norms for human conduct. In a recent and useful discussion of this issue, Richard Bauckham points out that, at one level, the Bible does claim to offer an interpretative framework for understanding the divine will for all people (2003, pp. 87-88). However, he argues, there is also another side to this. The Bible is *not* a "totalising" system, of the kind that Lyotard attacks. Bauckham suggests that better examples of oppressive totalising systems are Marxist economics, global capitalism, the myth of scientific progress, and what he calls the Americanisation of the world (p. 89). The Bible, on the other hand, does not bring oppression; it brings liberation.

Further, Bauckham points out that, far from offering a single monolithic "grand narrative" of all history, the biblical material bubbles with numerous "little" narratives: tales about particular persons in particular places at particular times, through whom God performs particular acts. He rightly observes that, in positive terms, Lyotard's hostility to universals can remind us that the Bible and biblical interpretation take place within a dialectic between unity and diversity, between coherence and particularity, between grand narrative and little narrative. The Bible does speak of God's universal purposes for the world, and of creation and human destiny, but it also addresses me in my situation, and everyday people in everyday life. A constructive untidiness, he argues, characterises the Bible and its meanings.

Can the Bible Mean Whatever We Want It to Mean?

In practice, there is a darker side to Lyotard than Bauckham acknowledges. Lyotard's belief that "difference" is irresolvable without one party's assimilation of the other into its conceptual frame to take control leads him to reject any quest for *criteria*. *Criteria, he insists, are oppressive*. Hence, in effect, he rejects the agenda of hermeneutics and of this lecture. We are concerned to seek reasonable criteria for interpretation. Nevertheless, Bauckham's response concerning the Bible remains valid. His dialectic characterizes Christian theology and hermeneutics as such.

I shall illustrate this from a university in which I have taught for the last twelve years. Colleagues in the Department of Philosophy and colleagues in the School of Critical Theory have privately expressed to me their intense disenchantment with the other Department. To many philosophers, critical theory's hospitality to postmodernism seems to transpose philosophy into sociology. What shapes human thought is said to be the social, contingent conditioning of race, class, gender, historical period, and economic interest. On the other hand, many critical theorists confide to me that, in their view, the philosophers deal in unreal abstractions, divorcing thought from the particularities of life that shape and even determine it.

Nevertheless, I have been made welcome in *both* Departments as a teacher and research supervisor. Philosophers know that theology speaks of a Creator God who transcends this or that race, class, and historical era, that it seeks rational coherence and that it explores theories of knowledge and ontology. Conversely, critical theorists know that, in teaching and using biblical texts, we pay every attention to historical and contingent factors to shape horizons of interpretation and that we focus on Jesus of Nazareth, who was a first-century Jew, born into the social and economic conditions of a specific time. Indeed, as the theologian Eberhard Jüngel observes, God is "conceivable" because Jesus Christ articulates God in temporal and bodily modes (1983, pp. 152-169).

(2) Our second point concerns *contextualization*. Few stress the importance of textual and situational contexts more strongly than biblical specialists. However, there is a difference between the valid insight that all meanings are contextually *conditioned and constrained,* and a radical claim that no criterion of meaning can extend *beyond the horizons of this or that "local community" of readers.* Richard Rorty and Stanley Fish promote this internalism within the framework of American neo-pragmatic postmodernity. There is no criterion of meaning and truth beyond what a given community finds conducive to its progress.

Rorty writes: "There is no Way the World is". There is no such task as "getting reality right". The only currency of the word "true" is simply "what can be justified" and "justification is *always relative to an audience*" (1998, pp. 4 and 25). But this "audience" is Rorty's own community of readers. No trans-contextual or external criteria of meaning and truth exist.

This approach undermines not only epistemology, but also hermeneutics, although Rorty claims to reinvent hermeneutics as "not a 'method for attaining truth'", but a way of "coping with the world" (1979, pp. 359 and 365). The notion that "there is *one right way*" of meaning or understanding owes more, he says, to misdirected intuition than to reflection (p. 375). Rorty shares with Stanley Fish the view that what *counts as* valid truth, interpretation, meaning or understanding can be determined only in

## Can the Bible Mean Whatever We Want It to Mean?

relation to slots in the pre-existing horizons of a community of interpreters. I contend that this reverses the purpose of hermeneutics, and turns the work of Gadamer and Ricoeur on its head.

I have criticized these views at length elsewhere, not least in Nottingham University's School of Critical Theory. In short, Rorty relies too heavily upon a radically pluralist interpretation of the philosophy of language in the later Wittgenstein, and an overstated and exaggerated dependence upon a notion of "incommensurability" drawn from the earlier work of Thomas Kuhn in the philosophy of science. In addition to my own published contributions, Jane Heal (1990) criticises Rorty's understanding of Wittgenstein, and Georgia Warnke (1987, pp. 146-156) and Stephen Fuller (2003) show the un-wisdom of any over-dependence on incommensurability in the earlier work of Kuhn.

Rorty and Fish, then, answer the question: "Can the Bible mean whatever we want it to mean?" in their own terms, with a resounding "Yes". However their "Bible" is a virtual reality constructed by self-affirming consumerist profiles. In my commentary on 1 Corinthians, I point out that Paul emphatically rejects the notion of a Gospel redefined by consumerist expectations and audience demands (1 Cor. 1: 18-25). I have also argued that Rorty and Fish base their work on illusory premises and mistaken arguments in their philosophy of language.

(3) On a third point, however, European postmodernism and the biblical writings share one common theme. Both emphasise the capacity of the human heart for self-deception and for a ready use of disguise for purposes of self-affirmation and the manipulation of others. Allusions to the deceitfulness of the human heart

## Can the Bible Mean Whatever We Want It to Mean?

occur in the Old Testament and in the New. Gerd Theissen gives an excellent exposition of this dimension in Paul's theology in his *Psychological Aspects of Pauline Theology* (1987). Among postmodern writers, Michel Foucault builds on the earlier work of Nietzsche, emphasising how disguise plays its part in institutional regimes, including hospitals, prisons, the armed services and the Church. Often, several of these secure "docility" by means of what Foucault calls "the smiling face in a white coat" (1977; cf. further 1988-1990). (He does not mention the smiling face in the clerical collar).

In contrast to the postmodernity of American pragmatism, I argue that European postmodernism can provide the biblical interpreter with positive resources for diagnosing examples of inauthentic manipulation in the use of the Bible. According to Deuteronomy, the sin of failing to communicate the word of God is less serious only than the sin of attributing to God what God has not spoken, to serve self-interest.

(4) Finally, in those versions of literary postmodernity that follow Jacques Derrida on textuality, we face claims concerning the alleged instability of texts and meanings, and their disengagement with what Julia Kristeva calls "the speaking subject" (1973, pp. 1249-1252; 1986, pp. 25-32). The disappearance of the author may appear to present less serious problems for those kinds of texts that Lotman and Eco call "productive" or "open" texts. The Book of Jonah might just possibly provide such an example, since it functions virtually as a self-contained narrative in its own right. Even so, only certain parts of the biblical writings are texts of this kind, and hardly the majority.

Can the Bible Mean Whatever We Want It to Mean?

As Paul Ricoeur observes, the Bible embodies at least five types of texts. These include hymnic, narrative, and wisdom texts, but in addition to these it embodies *prophetic and didactic* texts. At the very least in the case of the latter two, to separate the text from its prophetic or apostolic authority is to destroy a good part of what the text amounts to. The later Wittgenstein observes that communicative action, or the language-game, is very often "the whole, consisting of language and the actions into which it is woven" (1953, section 7). I have offered an extensive critique of Derrida's theory of texts in *New Horizons in Hermeneutics* (1992), and updated comments will appear in 2005 in the volume *Thiselton on Hermeneutics: Collected Works* (in press).

Archbishop Rowan Williams makes some incisive comments on this theory of texts in his essay "Hegel and the gods of postmodernity" (in Berry & Wernick, 1992). In the end, Williams observes, the Bible would become a speechless void: "There are no *words* of grace" (p. 73). Jüngel further insists, as we have noted, that the "embodiment" of God in Christ is what makes God "thinkable" and "speakable". The *word* was made *flesh*. As Wittgenstein observes, we learn linguistic currencies by watching how speakers live and act: "One learns the game by watching how others play" (1953, section 54).

To respond to the question: "Can the Bible mean whatever we want it to mean?" requires patience, openness, listening, understanding and, indeed, for a serious answer, the full repertoire of hermeneutics, as well as these hermeneutical virtues. I hope that I may have signposted some fruitful ways forward, but I had never expected to offer a comprehensive response within an hour. To claim to have offered a comprehensive package

Can the Bible Mean Whatever We Want It to Mean?

as a response to such a complex question would invite legitimate suspicion that I had merely set before you some doctrinaire metanarrative of a closed, pre-determined, sterile, scholastic, system. This was not my goal.

**References**

Alter, R. (1981). *The art of biblical narrative*. London: Allen & Unwin.

Alves, R. (1969). *A theology of human hope*. New York: Corpus Books.

Bakhtin, M. M. (1973). *Problems of Dostoevsky's poetics* (R.W. Rotsel, Trans.). Ann Arbor, MI: Ardis. (Original work published 1929).

Barr, J. (1980). Has the Bible any authority? In J. Barr, *The scope and authority of the Bible* (pp. 52-64). London: SCM Press.

Bauckham, R. (2003). *Bible and mission: Christian witness in a postmodern world*. Carlisle: Paternoster Press.

Betti, E. (1967). *Allgemeine Auslegungslehre als Methodik des Geisteswissenschaften*. Tübingen: Mohr. (Original work published 1955).

Betti, E. (1972). *Die Hermeneutik als allgemeine Methodik des Geisteswissenschaften*. (2nd ed). Tübingen: Mohr. (Original work published 1962).

Can the Bible Mean Whatever We Want It to Mean?

Chatman, S. (1978). Story and discourse: Narrative structure in fiction and film. Ithaca, NY: Cornell University Press.

Church of England, Doctrine Commission of the General Synod. (2003). *Being human: A Christian understanding of personhood illustrated with reference to power, money, sex and time.* London: Church House Publishing.

Culler, J. (1981). The pursuit of signs: Semiotics, literature, deconstruction. London: Routledge & Kegan Paul.

Culler, J. (1975). *Structuralist poetics: Structuralism, linguistics and the study of literature.* London: Routledge & Kegan Paul.

Dodd, C. H. (1928). *The authority of the Bible.* London: Nisbet.

Dostoevsky, F. M. (1976). *The brothers Karamazov* (C. Garnett, Trans.). New York: Norton. (Original work published 1879-1880).

Eco, U. (1979). *The role of the reader: Explorations in the semiotics of texts.* Bloomington: Indiana University Press.

Eco, U. (1984). *Semiotics and the philosophy of language.* London: Macmillan.

Fish, S. (1989). Introduction: Going down the anti-formalist road. In S. Fish, *Doing What Comes Naturally: Change, Rhetoric, and the Practice of Theory In Literary and Legal Studies* (pp.1-33). Oxford: Clarendon Press.

Foucault, M. (1977). *Discipline and punish: The birth of the prison* (A. Sheridan, Trans.). New York: Pantheon Books. (Original work published 1975).

Foucault, M. (1978-86). *The history of sexuality* (R. Hurley, Trans.). (3 vols.). New York: Pantheon Books. (Original work published 1976-84).

Fuller, S. (2003). Kuhn vs. Popper: The struggle for the soul of science. Cambridge: Icon.

Gadamer, H.-G. (1989). *Truth and method* (J. Weinsheimer & D. G. Marshall, Trans. Rev.). (2$^{nd}$ ed.). London: Sheed & Ward. (Original work published 1960).

Genette, G. (1980). *Narrative discourse* (J. E. Lewin, Trans.). Ithaca, NY: Cornell University Press. (Original work published 1972).

Heal, J. (1990). Pragmatism and choosing to believe. In A. R. Malachowski (Ed.), *Reading Rorty: Critical responses to philosophy and the mirror of nature (and beyond)* (pp. 101-114). Oxford: Basil Blackwell.

Hopkins, J. H. (1864). *A scriptural, ecclesiastical, and historical view of slavery: From the days of the patriarch Abraham to the nineteenth century.* New York: W. I. Pooley & Co.

Irenaeus. (1885). Against heresies (A. Roberts & W. H. Rambaut, Trans.). In A. Roberts & J. Donaldson (Eds.), A. C. Coxe (Rev.), *The Ante-Nicene Fathers: Translations of the writings of the Fathers down to A. D. 325* (vol. 1, pp. 315-567). Grand Rapids, MI: Wm. B. Eerdmans. (Original work written ca. 180-200).

Jüngel, E. (1983). God as the mystery of the world: On the foundation of the theology of the Crucified One in the dispute between theism and atheism (D. L. Guder, Trans.). Edinburgh: T & T Clark. (Original work published 1977).

Knight, G. W. (1975). Can a Christian go to war? *Christianity Today, 20* (4), 4.

Kristeva, J. (1973, October 12). The system and the speaking subject. *The Times Literary Supplement*, pp.1249-1252.

Can the Bible Mean Whatever We Want It to Mean?

Reprinted: In T. Moi (Ed.). (1986). *The Kristeva reader* (pp. 25-32). New York: Columbia University Press.

Lotman, J. (1977), *The structure of the artistic text* (R. Vroon, trans.). Ann Arbor: University of Michigan. (Original work published 1971).

Lundin, R., Walhout, C., & Thiselton, A. C. (1999). *The promise of hermeneutics.* Grand Rapids, MI: W. B. Eerdmans.

Lyon, D. (1994). *Postmodernity.* Buckingham: Open University Press.

Lyotard, J.-F. (1984). *The postmodern condition: A report on knowledge* (G. Bennington & B. Massumi, (Trans.). Manchester: Manchester University Press.

Mofokeng, T. (1988). Black Christians, the Bible and liberation. *Journal of Black Theology in South Africa, 2* (1), 34-42.

Morgan, R. (1988). *Biblical interpretation.* Oxford: Oxford University Press.

Nietzsche, F. (1990). *Twilight of the idols, and The Antichrist* (R. J. Hollingdale, Trans.). London: Penguin Books. (Original works published 1889, 1895).

Pannenberg, W. (1971), *Basic questions in theology, vol. 2* (G. H. Kehm, Trans.). London: SCM Press. (Original work published 1967).

Räisänen, H. (2001). The New Testament in theology. In H. Räisänen, *Challenges to Biblical interpretation: Collected essays 1991-2001* (pp. 227-249). Leiden: Brill.

Ricoeur, P. (1970). *Freud and philosophy: An essay in interpretation* (D. Savage, Trans.). New Haven, CT: Yale University Press. (Original work published 1965).

Ricoeur, P. (1992). *Oneself as another* (K. Blamey, Trans.). Chicago: University of Chicago Press. (Original work published 1990).

Rorty, R. (1979). *Philosophy and the mirror of nature.* Princeton, NJ: Princeton University Press.

Rorty, R. (1998). *Truth and progress.* Cambridge: Cambridge University Press.

Schleiermacher, F. (1977). *Hermeneutics: The handwritten manuscripts* (H. Kimmerle (Ed.; J. Duke & J. Forstman Trans.). Missoula, MT: Scholars Press, for the American Academy of Religion. (Original work written 1805-1829; this edition originally published 1959).

Can the Bible Mean Whatever We Want It to Mean?

Searle, J. R. (1983). *Intentionality: An essay in the philosophy of mind.* Cambridge, Cambridge University Press.

Theissen, G. (1987). *Psychological aspects of Pauline theology* (J. P. Galvin, Trans.). Philadelphia: Fortress Press. (Original work published 1983).

Thiselton, A. C. (1980). *The two horizons: New Testament hermeneutics and philosophical description with special reference to Heidegger, Bultmann, Gadamer, and Wittgenstein.* Exeter: Paternoster Press.

Thiselton, A. C. (1992). *New horizons in hermeneutics: The theory and practice of transforming biblical reading.* Grand Rapids, MI: Zondervan.

Thiselton, A. C. (1995). *Interpreting God and the postmodern self: On meaning, manipulation and promise.* Edinburgh: T & T Clark.

Thiselton, A. C. (2000). *The first epistle to the Corinthians: A commentary on the Greek text.* Grand Rapids, MI: W. B. Eerdmans.

Thiselton, A. C. (in press). *Thiselton on hermeneutics: Collected works.* Aldershot: Ashgate.

Ward, G. (2001). Introduction: "Where we stand". In G. Ward (Ed.), *The Blackwell Companion to Postmodern Theology* (pp. xii-xxvii). Oxford: Blackwell.

Warnke, G. (1987). *Gadamer: Hermeneutics, tradition and reason.* Cambridge: Polity Press.

Williams, R. (1992). Hegel and the gods of postmodernity. In P. Berry & A. Wernick (Eds.), *Shadow of spirit: Postmodernism and religion* (pp. 72-80). London: Routledge.

Wittgenstein, L. (1953). *Philosophical investigations* (G. E. M. Anscombe, Trans.). Oxford: Blackwell.